THEY CALL ME 'COACH E'

Leading to Achieve the Unachievable

Bill Edson

Amazon-Kindle Direct Publishing

Copyright © 2020 Bill Edson

All rights reserved

The characters and events portrayed in this book are fictitious. Any similarity to real persons, living or dead, is coincidental and not intended by the author.

No part of this book may be reproduced, or stored in a retrieval system, or transmitted in any form or by any means, electronic, mechanical, photocopying, recording, or otherwise, without express written permission of the publisher.

ISBN-13: 9798653154492

Cover design by: Art Painter
Library of Congress Control Number: 2018675309
Printed in the United States of America

To my wife, Carol, who always loves, supports, and believes in me unconditionally.

To my Mom, who had a passion for the written word, and by writing this book, I have fulfilled both of our dreams.

To all my athletes who constantly inspire me, make me laugh or cry, but always give me purpose greater than myself.

And, to my daughter, Nina, who kept me from making the biggest mistake of my life.

"Coach E has made a profound impact on the athletes in our little town. They never even dreamed of what they could achieve, and the kind of success they have had in such a short amount of time."

- Elise, parent

"Mr. Edson's passion is coaching. His pride and joy is seeing his athletes succeed. He knows how to push his athletes while also being supportive and inspiring. When I would celebrate a new PR, he was right there with me celebrating alongside me! When I was feeling down about my race outcome, he always had the words to lift me back up for next time!"

-Kelly, former athlete

"...all the moments I have had being under your wing as an athlete, and friend, I have loved and will always cherish, you have been someone I have looked up to and in all moments of you coaching me, have learned, loved and appreciated immensely.... you pushed me to be the best I could be..."

-Ethan, current athlete

"Because of you, I learned how to push myself mentally and physically, trust in my abilities, have confidence and strive to be the best version of me."

-Myka, former athlete

"To me, there is not enough words to describe what you have accomplished with your life. From your high school days, serving your country, community and becoming a truly outstanding Coach and mentor. I wish you continued success and can't wait to read your book."

-Coach Stricker, Coach E's former high school coach

PREFACE

As I stood behind the starting line and watched the seven boys quickly remove their warm-ups and reveal their top-secret black uniforms, the steam wafted in the cold Fall air from their shoulders as they toed the line in preparation for the start of their run into history. It was the start of the race, the beginning of a new legacy, but it was the end of a year-long journey of discovering excellence and denying mediocrity. It was the summation from days of hard work, thousands of miles, and hours of planning, strategizing, and relationship building. Why was this team, that only one year prior, was seen as a competitive doormat but now on the doorstep to unprecedented success?

As they say, this was "not my first rodeo" when it came to lifting a team to new heights of what could be described as "over-achieving". I prefer to explain it as discovering victory, achieving the unachievable. It is something that I have done for years, time and time again, not just within the realm of athletics as a coach, but as an organizational executive, a military leader, and a father as well. This book will be filled with the pearls of wisdom that nearly three decades of being a successful leader and coach have collected. Experiences that can be applied to any venue of leadership be it coaching, business, the military, organizational administration, church groups, or even family, my passion for coaching athletes and helping them become better humans has always floated to the top as my purpose...a purpose greater than myself...it is what drives me... and, at this stage of my life I have decided it is worth sharing. Not because I am in search of some superficial notoriety or vain validation but because by sharing, it just may help to make this world a better place...my ultimate goal. One person at a time if need be. And now, after reading, perhaps you will join me and help with that goal.

SECTION I – MY BASICS

"I love those who can smile in trouble, who can gather strength from distress, and grow brave by reflection. 'Tis the business of little minds to shrink, but they whose heart is firm, whose conscience approves their conduct, will pursue their principles unto death"

-Leonardo da Vinci

GOLDEN BUZZER MOMENTS

◆ ◆ ◆

I find myself a covert fan of the popular show 'America's Got Talent' (and 'Britain's Got Talent' too). I typically view it late at night, in bed, wearing headphones as not to bother my wife while she sleeps beside me. It's not the weekly television show per se, but the highlights that I can find on YouTube that I love. Specifically, the 'Golden Buzzer' highlights. If you are not familiar with this program, it is a variety contest where every day common folks get the opportunity to exhibit their talents to a panel of celebrity judges, on stage, and in front of a massive crowd of on-lookers. Sometimes the talent is okay, sometimes weird, sometimes awful. But sometimes it is amazing beyond description and the judges reward those auditioning by pressing the 'Golden Buzzer' and launching them straight to the final rounds of the competition. It is a joyful and remarkable moment for the entertainers...a breakthrough moment that is celebrated with cheers and congratulations, music, flashy gold confetti, and plenty of emotion, They earned it and I often find myself in tears as I witness them achieving, what only a few moments previously they believed, as the unachievable.

Why do I find this so appealing? It certainly is not because I am an entertainer, or even seek some sort of heightened celebrity or fast track to the top. Instead because I can relate to their journeys. The time, work, passion, and efforts that they dedicated towards pursuing nothing but a dream…the intangible and often unachievable vision that they cling to as they endure more setbacks and disappointment throughout that quest than most people would tolerate. Yet, they keep going because of the dream. It is so often not about the performers either but about their stories. The episodes that truly touch my soul are the performers that win for someone else…in the name of a child, a parent, their family, a cause, a profound purpose…all greater than themselves. It is this that I truly relate and when I witness this kind of genuine achievement, I am internally elated within the witnessing of them discovering this type of victory.

Now, don't get me wrong, I am not lost in this as a rainbow and unicorn fantasy moment of 'all is well that ends well'. The reality of this achievement is that it is often met with yet another heart-wrenching defeat in the finals, as only one contestant will win the whole thing. But it's that moment that I yearn for, not so much for me (although honestly, deep down, there is a selfish yearning…who doesn't like to win?), but for my athletes. I want them to be able stand at the top of a podium and be empowered by the emotion and satisfaction of the moment. I want them to have that memory and use it as a driving force to get beyond the next letdown in life, so they can keep moving forward with that valuable momentous tool in their pocket. So, I guess, the 'golden buzzer' moments give me a quick fix of hope to keep me going too, for my athletes' and my own unachievable visions.

IT STARTS SOMEWHERE

◆ ◆ ◆

It was never my intention to be a coach. Now, nearly 3 decades later, it has become my most meaningful vocation and something that I cannot even imagine navigating life without.

I was born and raised in a small mill town in Northern New York State. In fact, the closet major metropolis to my hometown was Montreal…Canada. I lived a typical all-American boy's life. I had wonderful parents, a couple of siblings, and terrific grandparents. I went to church every Sunday and we ate at the dinner table as a family every evening. My dad was a papermaker and my mom worked as a secretary for a local museum. It was a modest and fairly typical lifestyle. Sports were a huge influence in my life. I played Little League baseball and learned the value of practice and the gains that can come from putting in the work. I played nearly every position but fell in love with pitching. I was attracted to the idea of going one on one with my opponents…to outwit them and over power them was very satisfying to me and it planted the seed of my competitiveness, that over time, grew into a strong oak of a fierce attitude to achieve.

Once Little League was over as I entered Middle School, I began to run. My brother was a very good runner and my dad ran in high school, and I loved his stories. We watched the Olympic games and followed the track and field athletes like most kids follow the Yankees or the Red Sox. My first race was a 9-mile road race from Elizabethtown to Westport where I won a trophy for being the youngest finisher...probably the only time that I got a trophy and my brother did not.

I was the middle child of the three of us. Whether it is simply speculation or not, I felt like that dynamic also had fostered my strong sense of independence and competitiveness. I felt like I had to work harder to gain the same attention that was granted to my superstar brother and my younger princess sister.

My brother was an amazing High School runner and a good inspiration for me. I remember the large clothing box under his bed full of college recruiting letters. He went undefeated his final two years in high school cross country and although a quiet person, he was a fierce competitor. However, it was a tough standard and did present some pressure for me to also be a good runner. It was no secret, I was NOT my brother, and frankly, not a particularly good runner as a Freshman in high school. It did not come naturally for me but with determination and support from my parents and my brother, my coaches, and allot of hard work, I made myself into a very competitive athlete and a top runner in our conference for both cross country and track and field by the time I graduated.

I did not receive any recruiting offers and decided to compete collegiately as a walk-on for the cross country team at Cortland State University. In brief, the experience was not a positive one but still profoundly valuable. I was not treated fairly or respectfully, and unlike my coaches in high school, the coach was an example of how not to coach or lead a team, and the upper classmen were pompous bullies. However, that environment sparked my resolve to achieve, perhaps more by competitive vengeance than anything else.

But what I always came back to was the success of my high school team. Remember that "momentous tool" of experience that I mentioned earlier? Our cross country team (emphasis on 'our') was very good and our track team was very good too. Collectively, we won 7 out of 8 conference or section championships during my four years in high school. Often beating teams from schools that were two or three times the size of ours. And, it was those memories of achieving collectively, at times when it was even deemed unachievable by many, that I have always, and still do hold in my pocket as inspiration to keep working, even if the outcome may appear to be unachievable at face value. Because, realizing once the unachievable has been achieved, then anything is possible. That is the power of that 'tool' in your pocket and the basis to why I am so driven as a coach to provide that same 'momentous tool' to my athletes. It is a tool they will carry with them in life, well beyond sports, and will allow them to keep battling, keep working, keep moving forward just as it has for me during life's most challenging moments (and I have had more than my share) where the easiest solution would be to simply give up. No, instead I reach into my pocket and pull out the memory of achieving the unachievable, so I keep moving, keep working, and rally to discover the victory within the circumstance, and to keep moving forward. For me, coaching is not to collect wins or loses, it is to teach critical lessons of life that will shape young people to be resilient and responsible human beings. However, the "tool" is the gift that comes from the treasured memory of achieving above all others on the field of competition and beyond your own expectation, whatever that may look like to you.

MAKING CHICKEN SALAD

♦ ♦ ♦

When I was in Basic Training after I joined the United States Army, I remember one of my Drill Sergeants making this statement upon arriving at boot camp, "I am tasked with the impossible task. It is my job to make you all into soldiers. It's like making chicken salad out of chicken shit."

I cannot help but think that this saying perfectly sums up my job as a coach. Now, before you get your panties all up in a bunch, what I am NOT saying is that those I coach are equivalent to that of chicken excrement.

Remember this, number 1; This is only

a saying and within any saying there is meaning. Number 2; Do not get all emotional about things. As a coach, you have assumed a serious responsibility as a real leader.

This requires real leader skills to which one is having the ability to filter out emotion within your tasks as a coach. I am not saying that you should ignore or discredit emotions, emotions can be an especially important element of the coaching experience. What I am saying is that you must filter them, control them, and never make a decision, judgment, or statement based purely on emotion. In the leadership world, this is called emotional intelligence. It is the ability to recognize and measure emotions in order to maintain control of the environment in which you are leading. Emotions can be the critical tool that will help inspire your athletes to victory or discourage them into defeatism.

Now, back to the meaning of the saying. One part of why I love coaching is that every year, every season, the dynamics of building a team is different. Not one season is the same. Even if you have the same kids, changes occur within the dynamic of those athletes that create new challenges or offer fresh possibilities. It is like an artist who would be handed a blank canvas or a lump of clay and then have the ability to create it into a masterpiece painting or beautiful sculpture. It is simply taking the raw material that has been handed to you and then making something special from it... maybe not as crass as chicken excrement, but the same principle in meaning.

In January 2005, I arrived at Camp Shelby, Mississippi as the Senior Medical Non-Commissioned Officer in charge of the medical section for my battalion. It was my job to lead and prepare a group of US Army National Guardsmen to deploy and render medical care on the battlefields of Iraq. Arguably, it was my biggest and most important coaching challenge of my career. As a member of the National Guard, I was called to this duty and was expected to take a diverse band of '"misfit" civilian soldiers and turn them into a cohesive unit of warriors who could save lives while under the most austere conditions.

To be clear, it was not that these people were personally unable, it was that I was handed a lump of cold clay to mold into a masterpiece sculpture. It was a chicken shit scenario and I had no other option but to make chicken salad. I knew some of these soldiers but for the most part, I did not really know them, or understand their capacities and abilities as soldiers or as medics. I had a group of 51 men (and eventually three women) ranging from 19 to 54 years old, who came from 10 different states, and represented every ethnic and social description that could be presented. I needed to create, in essence, a championship team from what I was given. Well, isn't this as coaches, what we are expected to do each and every season? In short, and in my mind, the quick answer is a resounding, YES.

So, how do I do it time and time again? Well it's a combination of understanding the recipe and assembling the ingredients, when mixed, it makes the most delicious chicken salad that was ever eaten. The rest of this book will provide some of these ingredients and we will unpack them at deeper levels.

For now, there are some critical things to consider as ingredients. What is the culture of your team? What about its overall temperature of attitude and mindset? What are the resources that you have to create this masterpiece? And perhaps, what is your capability as a leader to develop a strategy and carry it out towards the objectives of your program? Keep reading and I bet you will have an opportunity to explore these things, and more.

So, how did it turn out for my "misfit" medics? Well, after months of training, establishing a culture of winners and warriors, building genuine relationships, understanding our strengths and weaknesses, making tough decisions, creating allegiances, applying innovative solutions, and overcoming immense hardships it turned out pretty well.

In the end, this chicken shit band of misfitted soldiers performed over 5,000 medical missions on the battlefield, 100% of them individually earned the esteemed Combat Medical Badge. As part of a high-stakes Army unit that served with the United States Marine Corps they received two awards for honorable service in combat from the United States Navy. And as a team, they became a renowned force of life-saving distinction during their 12-months of selfless service in the Iraq war. The Command Sergeant Major from the theater of operations described us this way, "If the Voodoo Medics can't save you, then there's nobody that can".

It was a remarkable tribute to my coaching philosophy, that when embraced and ingredients assembled, produced a gourmet chicken salad. How this plays out on the track or the trails with the development of successful teams will be further discussed throughout the book.

COACHING IS LEADING

◆ ◆ ◆

Before we even begin discussing your team and how to build it, let's talk about you, the coach. Let us fully understand that coaching is leading, and in order to lead successfully you should understand some key components of effective leadership and leader skills. This will be your foundation to building and coaching a successful program. Good, bad, or indifferent there is much truth in the belief that teams are a direct reflection of their coach. Your team will only be as capable as you are as a coach.

So first, what is leadership? By definition, Leadership is the ability to influence those around you to meet a common objective or goal. Sounds very "coachy" right from the start, right? I think the first key point to make here is that leading is NOT about YOU...nor is coaching. It is first and foremost about a common goal or objective that includes your purpose and ideals as a coach. This could be called and described as your coaching philosophy. It is the foundation of your program and your "why" for the reason you are coaching in the first place. It has nothing to do with collecting "w's" or winning championships. I am not saying that those things should not be a part of it, and in fact measuring successes through winning is very important, but if you are coaching for all the right reasons, those types of things are not part of the overall bigger picture as a coach.

I began coaching as a complete circumstance of necessity. I never had any real ambitions to be a coach. Our son was in 4th grade and we signed him up for a recreation basketball program. I am not a helicopter parent, so we would drop him off at the gym a couple of days each week and show up 2 hours later after practice and he would run out the door and jump in the car. Pretty typical scenario for youth basketball or youth sports in general in those days. In my mind, I was envisioning that he was receiving some instruction on the basics of the game, learning some skills, and benefitting from some positive structure that sports can offer. So, one day after a couple of weeks, I decided to show up early and check in on progress. When I walked into the gym, I could not believe my eyes! I did not walk into a gym…I stepped into a den of complete chaos and disorganization! There were forty-five 4th and 5th graders aimlessly running around the gym, balls flying back and forth, kids screaming and whistles blowing. It resembled more a combination of dodgeball and cat herding rather than the sport of basketball. In fact, I distinctly remember one of the kids literally hanging from the gym rafters above the basketball goal and the "coach" yelling, "Jimmy get down from there before you get hurt!". The volunteer college-aged "coaches" were obviously over their heads and the good intention of them helping with youth sports as community service was going horribly in the wrong direction.

So, without hesitation but with much trepidation, I contacted the Director of the recreation department and volunteered to take over the program. After it was all said and done, and seeing how guided structure, purposeful interaction, and having organized fun can positively impact our youth, I was hooked on coaching! The very next season, I was hired as a high school basketball coach and subsequently began coaching youth cross country and track too.

So, back to the topic of leadership. Why is this so important? Because real coaches are leaders and effective leaders make for great coaches and great coaches impact athletes well beyond the court, track, and trails. (Do you see the bigger purpose here?)

Let's first discuss some basic leader styles or types. There are four of them:

>**Authoritative** – Complete leader control and oversight. Your way or the highway.
>
>**Collaborative** – A cooperative partnership. Working together towards a common direction.
>
>**Democratic** – The followers dictate direction by majority input.
>
>**Laissez-faire** – Followers com-

pletely control and determine direction.

Which category do you fall into? While there may be elements of some of them, or all of them, within your leader / coaching style, the one style that you mostly embrace will have dramatic effect upon the results you see within your program. It will also have strong influence that you will play on the long-term impact of your athletes.

The fact is, maybe you are not in it for the long-term impact, you just want the wins. Perhaps you feel that the winning experience will impact the athletes. This may be true, but what is your priority? You see, I believe that winning is always a by-product of an overall healthy and effective program. In fact, winning by itself, is quite superficial. It is the deeper elements of the coach-athlete-team relationship that puts the positive impact into winning. As a track and cross country coach, I have seen coaches place emphasis on their superstar athlete and simply go thru the motions with the other kids. Sure, maybe the star ends up on the podium or as a state champion but the dynamic effect that you will have on your team, the other athletes, will not be positive or long lasting, nor will the team reach its potential. Ultimately, winning should not be the primary focus but just another measurable and attainable goal. Please don't get me wrong here, winning is fun and an important element for a successful program. It should just be kept in a healthy and motivational perspective...and of course celebrated. But winning is a matter of perspective and may not look like what you think it should look like. We will discuss that topic in another chapter.

Back to leader styles. Given the four leader styles as previously mentioned (Authoritarian, Collaborative, Democratic, and Laissez-faire) which do you feel is the most effective for successful coaching? It has been my observation and experience, having coached for nearly three decades, that the leader style that produces the most positive outcomes, by far, is the collaborative style of leadership. Within this style, relationships are made and trust is built between athletes and coaches. This is the very foundation of team culture, the key to a successful program (more on this later). It is the culture of a team that defines limitless behavior based on the selfless power of purpose rather than stifling attitude of selfishness.

Other leader skills that you must employ as a successful coach within the collaborative style of leadership are communication, emotional intelligence, empathy, and inclusivity.

Perhaps the most important skill any leader should employ is effective communication. Communication is the bonding element to all of your leader abilities. Think about it, it is what connects you with your coaching world. Everything that you interact with as a coach flows through your ability to communicate effectively. And just think of all the points of contact that you must form in order to create a successful program and all the formats that communication can be facilitated these days. Not only must you communicate with your athletes effectively, but the school or organizational administration, other coaches or a coaching association, the league or conference, the media, the public, the greater community of your sport, and especially...the parents!

And, then think about the many

means as how we communicate these days. Beyond the everyday in-person conversations, I maintain two social media sites, several texting groups, send home written memos, emails, memes, press releases, and have occasional team and parents meetings... and guess what? It' still not enough. It is essential to attempt every and all options to reduce the communication gap as much as possible. Transparency is paramount when developing a successful program. But let me also say this does not mean that you must divulge everything to the outside world. There is something to be said about maintaining what is sacred to your team. It is not about sharing everything either, it is about sharing essential information as appropriate to the party with whom you are communicating. Most importantly, remember this, communication is the dynamic of interchanging information. It is a two-way street. As long as you are keeping folks appropriately informed, in good faith, and understanding the input provided back to you, you will be fine, generally speaking. However, let me stress something extremely important, especially when communicating as a collaborative coach-leader...effective communication does not mean that you do all the talking. In fact, listening may be the more essential element of the whole equation of sharing information. Connecting with your athletes, at their level, and listening to them, observing body language, hearing, and seeing their cues and interactions, and asking open-ended questions will serve you best as their coach.

Subsequently, what you do with and how you react to the information that you receive, or share is dynamically important. Controlling the emotional temperature at those moments to control the atmosphere during what are so often tipping-point scenarios. Athletes are often fed or choked out by emotion, so you need to recognize it and understand your influential ability to control those moments deliberately or strategically through your behaviors and by the words you choose. This is called emotional intelligence.

I have a saying, "Perception is reality". Many people dispute this and argue that perception is not real, so therefore, it cannot be real. Well, perception is simply a matter of personal perspective, and it has been my experiential observation that if someone believes or perceives something to be real, the to them it is real. Therefore, it has the effect and impact of it actually being as such. Understanding this concept is a useful capability for a coach. Creating a positive perception can help to motivate or drive your athletes, but many times, false realities tend to restrict performance and hinder team output so that's what I want to address here. Typically, misperception is contrived by misinformation or miscommunication. Whether information was poorly communicated or simply not received as intended, it is important to understand that these moments all have a real basis of concern for the athlete. It is not simply a matter of dismissing it. If you want true resolution you must again open your ears and your mind as to why this perception exists in the first place. It requires listening but also putting yourself in the shoes of the person, or your team's perceived reality. It can be a frustrating situation so first, have the emotional restraint not to reflexively react to it. Instead, try to understand it because there is likely something real that triggered the belief. Show some compassion and patience, ask questions, address the situation with the truth, and clear the air. This is empathy at its essence. Being empathetic is not being weak, it is allowing yourself to connect and understand your athletes and your team at a deeper and more intimate level.

Finally, to make a long chapter even longer, let's talk about a concept that I call "inclusivity". This concept is particularly important as a collaborative leader. The word 'Collaborate", by Google's definition, means to "work together, especially to produce or create something". Not so much a coincidence that this definition sounds awfully close to the definition of leadership (The process of influencing others to achieve a common goal or objective.). And the bonding element that links collaboration and leadership is inclusivity. You see, coaching is a partnership between you, the coach, and your athletes. It is an individual partnership within a group partnership, made to achieve defined goals or objectives. But in order for it to be a true partnership, all / both parties must be included as participants in the process. This does not mean that all parties have equal or the same roles and responsibilities but understand that their role is valued and that they are appreciated, and as such, they feel that they are an essential part of the process, vision, and goals of the collaborative effort. With this understanding comes a sense of ownership to the program, and with that comes a commitment to it.

Also, a collaborative partnership offers opportunities to form real connections and relationships, and that's where real impact occurs. For instance, I often use video tape review to enhance training. I also depend on my partnership with my athletes to gain the most information possible in order to provide the best coaching direction. So, typically, I will video an athlete going through technique progressions and then share that video with the athlete in real time. Together, we review it, point out the good and the not-so-good, what needs improvement and how to improve it. Perhaps the most important element of this is that I take the time to ask the athlete about her opinion and feedback. How does she feel during the progression? What is she struggling with? What drills do you think will help? Then we can together proceed in a way to seek improvement of that skill on the same page, and with the same clear objectives in mind. Putting yourself in the shoes of this athlete, can you see how this would foster a respectful relationship, create a feeling that she is valued, and enhance her commitment to improvement, not to mention a strong sense of satisfaction and achievement when she sees improvement happening right in front of her eyes.

The bottom line is when someone is invested in the process, they are more likely to feel loyal, like they own it, and therefore work harder for it. Collaborative leadership is an efficient and intimate process that pays off in positive dividends with team dedication and positive performance results.

THE POWER OF CONNECTION

◆ ◆ ◆

Let us talk a little bit about the power of genuine human connection.

You will never reach your potential as a coach if you do not understand how to, and then employ, practices that will enhance your connection with your athletes and others associated with your program. A "just do it because I said so" approach may bring some superficial results, but it will pale in comparison to the positive impact you will have as a leader if you are truly connected. I am not saying that you have to be the kids' newest best friend but connected in a way that allows for a greater understanding of who each of you are, and therefore a discovery of the "why" you are in this together.

Let me be clear, when I say 'connected' it is more than a superficial acquaintance or transactional relationship between coach and athlete, leader and follower. It is the means that you genuinely join in a bonding element of trust where the purpose of your participation is performing for that other person on behalf of the commonalities and mutual respect that you have discovered. This type of connection takes voluntary and deliberate effort from you, as the coach. Naturally, the coach-athlete relationship is initially awkward and laced with barriers. It will be up to you to break through the awkwardness and break down those barriers. You will need to allow yourself to be in a position of vulnerability yet prove personal strength and competence by your natural actions, your openness, and your knowledge. Also, realize that gaining the type of genuine connection of which I am speaking is typically not a step by step procedure or universally check-the-box exercise that fits everyone the same. It really is a behavior mechanism that is recognized by your counterpart and evolves into a growing and mutually respectful relationship that is interactive at parallel levels. Admittedly, that sounds a bit wordy. None the less, your ability to successfully and genuinely connect with your athletes, parents, administrators, coaching colleagues, the media, the local community, et cetera will all prove to be paramount to the effort of achieving the unachievable for the sake of those you coach.

So, here are a five key pearls of wisdom to enhance your efforts to genuinely connect and build those important relationships.

1. Communicate effectively. Ask open-ended questions and listen. You will learn more and understand those whom you seek a relationship with, and therefore be able to position yourself in that common place where human connection can occur.

2. Allow yourself to be vulnerable. In other words, let yourself be seen as the genuine person that you are. This can be a challenge for some because the façade of being 'the tough coach that gets results' is often disingenuous and easier to maintain rather than actually working to gain the human connection that will create a deeply impactful true relationship. It may require you to open yourself up a little so that you become a real and relatable person within the dynamic of this two-way interchange. I am not saying that you share your deep dark secrets or most intimate personal feelings. But instead, allowing yourself to be seen as a fellow-human that will open doors between you and your team. One effective way that I like to foster connection is through the power of storytelling. I am not talking about 'back in the day' bragging but sharing a life story that helps people to understand, respect, and relate to who you are, where you come from, and why you are with them at this point in time. I use story nearly every day to build and maintain my connection with my teams. It may be a profound story about when I was at war, a third-person sports story, or simply a one-liner parable to make a point of focus. Either way, it must be relatable and pertinent. "Don't speak just for the sake of expelling carbon dioxide, that's what breathing is for...". (I refer to this when kids are not listening).

3. You also must be honest when connecting with others. This does not mean you can be insensitive, so compassion and empathetic understanding plays a part too. I am known for my honest approach, and sometimes I need to be firm, but I am always fair in my honesty.

Admittedly, I am not perfect at it, and am willing to allow for apology if warranted, but sugar-coating the truth or falsifying intent can do more damage than it can good to a long-term meaningful coach-athlete relationship. So, I engage with honest input and maintain the expectation to receive honest feedback, without judgement or punity. This helps to keep communication channels open and relationships genuine. Listen and respond with an open ear, a shoulder to lean on, and a reply that is controlled, thoughtful, and responsible.

As a leader who has built a relationship, you will be subject to sharing the good, bad, and ugly perspectives and situations of your athletes. So, be prepared to deal with those circumstances without judgement. Often, you will be their best, and perhaps, only advocate in their life. This requires a sense of sanctity and confidence that needs to be respected. Of course, this said, I recommend that you fully understand the mandated reporter policies of your school or organization and how that applies to you as a coach.

4. It is critically important when fostering a genuine human connection that you make the effort to validate the connection and the person with whom you are building a relationship. Also understand that this process is perpetual. It's not like you reach a point of establishing a connection and then you just let it go. Much like a garden needs water and weeding to bear produce, a connection needs to be nourished and maintained. Or it too will dry up and wither away.

5. Gaining and maintaining a genuine human connection is not simply speaking to each other. It so often requires action, so connect by example. Have you ever heard the term "lead by example"? I'm sure most of you have, and as a leader it is necessary to bolster any relationship through your actions. Your athletes want to be ensured that you have their backs and that you care about them. And besides, they want to trust you. So, give them actionable reason that will make this type of compassionate trust more evident than ever. You can do this in several ways.

When speaking to an athlete, the most sensitive time is likely when you are coaching them and offering critical feedback. Do this with sensitivity but be direct, truthful, and positive. Use real language. I maintain what I call "the sandwich method". If I am working with a triple jumper, a very technique intensive event, I may engage that athlete with a conversation like this, "So, your first-phase was quite good, the second phase actually kind of sucked...it was way too short. But you finished very nicely. If you can keep that lead knee and foot up on your second phase, and then add in the first and last just as you did it...then you've got a great jump just waiting to happen."

Now understand this, using real language within any conversation is relevant based on the extent of what is deemed appropriate for you and that particular athlete. I am not saying that you should be throwing F-bombs all over the place to make yourself seem cool. I am simply saying that real language reflects a genuine intent to your relationship. Your language may need to change based on who you are speaking with and what they respond to best. But do you see what I did there? I sandwiched the criticism with two positive statements. Always start and end your critique with positive or encouraging input…always.

Another way to exhibit your connection, or lead by example, is to show your athletes that you are willing to do what you are asking them to do. You can accomplish this by sharing in their workout. Run with them, participate in a relay with them, do some stretching or core workouts with them. You do not have to compete with them. This is not about proving yourself by beating them, it is about earning their respect and trust by being involved with them.

Now, I am pushing 60 years old (I can't even believe that I am saying this because I don't feel 60 in my mind) and I do not have the ability to workout with my team as I did in past years. I am a disabled veteran and so my body limitations prevent me from actively participating with my team at a high level. None the less, I do it when, where, and how I can. Because of the genuine relationship I have with my athletes, they understand and appreciate my limitations so they recognize any effort that I give towards actively participating with them. Sometimes you just have to get creative with how you can participate with your team. I often ride a bike on their long road runs. This allows me to be involved in their workouts, and it also provides me an added advantage to be more mobile and accessible to all the team members much more than just running. I often stretch with them and sometimes statically demonstrate certain techniques as well. And, once in a while, when I jump into a relay workout and grab that baton, it is very meaningful and always met with positive reaction by my team.

Also, on the level of keeping things real, also keep things fun. Have a sense of humor and allow those athletes to enjoy themselves during the moments when they can. I am not saying to let your program become a clown show, but just keep things grounded, and humor can be a great outlet for that. When I was in combat, you can only imagine some of the circumstances that I and my soldiers were exposed to. We experienced the worst that humanity has to offer... death, destruction, and loneliness. It was never so evident how humor was our release during those incredibly challenging and austere circumstances. It kept stress under control and helped us to remain focused and connected.

The bottom and most simplistic line when exhibiting human connection, or leading by example, is adhering to "the golden rule". Treat your athletes just as you would like to be treated... equally and fairly. Put yourself in their shoes, be empathetic, use some common sense, and just be there for them as they work towards their goals, expectations, and dreams...both on and off the track and trails.

Oh, by the way, just to be crystal clear your support and leadership does not start and end with your practice and meet schedules. There is no time clock for a genuinely committed human connection. If you are coaching for the right reasons, you are in it with your athletes through thick and thin, 24/7. This is how you will create the lasting impact that will make your athletes better teammates, classmates, family members, friends, and parents.

SEE THE INVISIBLE

◆ ◆ ◆

As you connect more with your athletes, you will get to know them better, understand their nuances, recognize their interests, and perhaps discover some hidden talents and gifts. As a coach, you need to have the ability to see the invisible. Observe and notice the not-so-obvious whether it is hidden within a person or your program. I guarantee you this, there is always an invisible trait or advantage, and being genuinely connected will help you see it. The invisible is often hiding in the minute details, it is camouflaged by habits and routines, but it is likely present right in front of your face.

This book mainly focuses on the intangibles of my coaching philosophies and best practices, it does not include much for practical strategy and training advice, the X's and O's of our sport. (That could be another book within its own context.) There are some practical things to keep in mind when looking for that invisible advantage.

One thing is observing your athletes as they perform. Be it during warm-ups, practice, competing, or just goofing around in between, the invisible unseen gift will show up at some point. So be diligent in your observations because it may just show up periodically, when you least expect it, and you won't want to miss it when it does.

The other thing to keep in mind when you are observing your athletes is body-type. Like any other sport, in track and field, body-type is often a precluded advantage. Tall, lean, and powerful folks often make for good high jumpers and triple jumpers, even though those events are not that popular with kids (mostly due to a lack of exposure to them). A sprinter with strong endurance can make for a good middle distance runner even though they have never raced beyond 200 meters. You must be willing and able to recognize hidden talents, and develop them, in order to make the most for an athlete and that often creates the best results for your team. I think it is too often that a coach, especially from a small school, believes that his team could be more competitive if he just had more athletes join the program. This may be true, but it is also highly likely that you already have more resources than you realize and it's how you discover and then employ those resources that will matter.

Ok, so for example, one day year's ago,

I was at a track practice late in the season, the hurdlers were just finishing up their drills so the hurdles were still set up on track. Our sprinters were doing their cool downs following some interval training, and I noticed that one of my 400m guys jogged off of the turn and was hurdling the leftover hurdles with near perfect form. Now, he had been on the team for three years, and never once did I see him try hurdling or hear him express any interest in hurdling. He was a solid 400m man, a point scorer in smaller meets and our #5 on the 4x400m relay and everyone was content with that including him…until that day. I called him over, "Hey Tenzin, I didn't know you could hurdle." "Either did I, Coach", he said. "I just thought I would try it. It looked fun." Understanding his proven speed and now recognizing his invisible talent, I asked him the obvious question.

"What do you think about trying the 300M hurdles in a meet?" He said, "Sure!". So, after a few days of working out a training regimen, he was exhibiting split times that had him in the mix as a top performer in the state for that event. I entered him in the next meet, and he promptly and effortlessly qualified for the state championships with the 4th best seed time overall. Two weeks later, he came off the final turn, and with 100 meters to go, he passed all competitors and taking them all by surprise, won the race going away, becoming my first hurdler to earn a State Championship. Additonally, it allowed me to be more creative and flexible with my team strategy and as a result, along with some other individual unachievable achievements that day, it was the first time in school history that both the boys and girls teams finished in the top three in a state finals.

Seeing the invisible does not only pertain to your athletes. It also relates to you, as a coach.

You must have the strength, security, and ability to be objectively introspective to of your own abilities and circumstances. You must be honest and willing to seek and accept help when it is in the best interest of your program. Face the facts, you will never be successful at the highest level without some kind of help or support. All great coaches have great assistants. In addition, be willing to let go a little and get outside of your comfort zone as a coach. Recognize that there may be other people with talents around you that could exceed your own, or at least compliment you as to help you achieve the unachievable.

I have always been quite good at finding and inviting external resources inside my coach-leader loop in order to benefit my athletes and the overall program. The trick is to find the right person who will bring added value to your program. There are allot of nice people out there who want to help, and you should consider everyone for a positive role within your program, but a good assistant will bring something unique and necessary, and most importantly, share in your vision and intentions for the athletes whom you coach.

When I first arrived as the new head cross country and track coach at my current school, I inherited a program from a coach who completely ignored or avoided her available resources. I think a challenge that some coaches (and leaders) have is a personal insecurity that an assistant will have more knowledge and experience than you. I think it is natural to perhaps feel a little bit threatened by this dynamic, and so the tendency is to put distance between themselves and that resource. An impact coach will seek out those people to make her program and efforts more effective and influential, and subsequently more productive.

So, when I arrived, my invisible resource was not so invisible. He stuck out to me like a flashing neon beacon with fireworks blasting in the background. His son was on the team and perhaps inviting a parent to get involved as an assistant brings some justified trepidation. But, if you do it with measured and clear intent, effectively communicating expectations along the way, compatibility will be validated, one way or the other, in short order.

This parent clearly proved his competence and potential value to my program very early in our acquaintance. His assets and experiences filled several evident gaps in the program. He was a former NH State Champion, a member of a legacy running program within the state, had coached an elite youth level running club, and was one of the top regional master runners in New England. He also knew the history of the current program, was acquainted with the kids and they knew him too, he has a fun sense of humor, and as a former State Champion who won on the same course where the NH championships are still held, he knew winning course strategy for that specific course.

And, he shared in the passion and positive energy, and immediately embraced my philosophy and goals for the program. To be honest, I had to pull in the reigns a little bit occasionally because he would get overly exuberant and too ambitious at times. Yet, he was appreciative of the open oversight and constructive partnership we had for each other, and it has made him a better assistant coach, which made me a better head coach. Perhaps most importantly, he was a family man of proven integrity. A coach that I could allow my athletes to fully embrace and would benefit from having him as part of their lives too. He was less of an invisible discovery and more of an ignored gift and I appreciate what he brings to my program.

So, what has happened with this coaching partnership? Besides us becoming close friends, Chris Bernier and I have become arguably the best coaching duo in New Hampshire Cross Country and Track. Within our first two years of coaching together, we are well on the way of creating our own legacy program with top rankings and performances at the state, region, and national levels.

I will say this, with his strong background, especially in the distance running disciplines, it made us as a coaching staff a little redundant. Distance and middle distance are also my favorite discpline specialties to coach. However, I didn't see it as redundancy or as a needless resource, I saw it as opportunity to personally grow as a coach and make our teams deeper too. In cross country, we collaborate on workouts and while my assistant executes those workouts with the more elite runners, I work with developing the others and creating a winning culture. This is a beautiful syncopated effort that is strengthening the program simultaneously from both ends. It also affords me the time to really concentrate on strategy, researching courses, evaluating our competitors, and building community and school support for our program.

During the track and field season, our coaching partnership has allowed me to self-evaluate and subsequently improve as a knowledgeable and effective coach in my abilities within the field event disciplines and subsequently expanding our coaching capabilities. Again, resulting in a top contending program in the state.

Remember, I cannot say this enough, coaching is NOT really about YOU, it's about those you coach, those you impact as your athletes and as fellow humans. So, choose and delegate your help wisely and don't hesititate to make some-self sacrifices on behalf of your program.

That said, if that special person is simply not available, fill the gaps with people in smaller support roles until that invisible person emerges. Do the best that you can with what you have for resources, be innovative, and make it the best program possible without compromise to your philosophy and focus, all for the sake of your athletes.

CULTURE

◆ ◆ ◆

Have you ever heard the old adage about running, "Running is 80% mental and 20% physical"? Well, I don't disagree with its premise that both a physical and psychological component exists. It's just that I believe they exist as separate yet equally essential components, both requiring 100% concentration of effort and energy from both coaches and athletes.

And, it all starts within the foundations of your program's culture.

Culture, in this circumstance, can be described as the values, beliefs, attitudes, and behaviors shared by a team.

Understand also that there can be positive and negative cultures. How that culture is developed and cultivated is totally up to you as the coach-leader. It is 100% your responsibility, and in reality, it is the most important element of your program. It is the foundation from which everything will derive.

A negative or weak culture will reflect a mediocre program at best, while a strongly positive culture will produce an impactful and successful program. Where strategies and philosophies may shift to meet the needs of your team and athletes' individual talents and demands, your program culture should be inflexible. It is the one constant that allows you to make team adjustments without losing the continuity and integrity that defines your program. Culture defines and identifies you as a coach and provides your program the unique brand that it is.

Also understand, that your team will have a culture, whether you deliberately build it with strategic and ethical intent, or you simply allow it to evolve on its own. I will let you guess which option tends to offer the best and most consistent outcomes.

When I first arrived as the new head coach at my current school, the culture that had evolved was one that resembled more of a running club rather than a competitive varsity program. The coach exhibited a more lassiez-faire leadership style and allowed the athletes to determine or highly influence workouts and team behavioral norms. It was a "just show-up" culture and whatever happens, happens attitude. Let me say, it has been my experience whether it is coaching sports, running an organization, or leading troops in battle, people want and appreciate structure and purpose. And they thrive on it, actually. Where culture is the foundation of your program, structure and purpose is the bedrock from which your culture and program are built.

It was very clear to me, right from the onset, that the program that I had inherited, had no specific structure nor strongly established purpose. Its performance history was mediocre with finishes at the state championships unimpressive. The kids felt unvalidated as athletes and they felt like their sport was not respected as a "real" varsity sport within the school community. And there was allot of truth to their perspectives. Other teams did not respectfully fear this program but often treated it as a participatory doormat, and saw it as a team that would simply show up to meets for the sake of showing up and could be used for their own development to trial strategy or enhance workouts.

Twenty minutes down the road is our rival school, and this school has a highly productive cross country legacy. They possess a strong history of success and have won many state championships which I greatly respect. The coach has a strong and confident personality, to a point of perceived arrogance, and his team follows suit.

He reached out to me early on, after I was hire, and began to dictate how the relationship between our programs have been in the past, as if I would simply continue in this passive trend for his benefit. It was as if we had an inferior program and our athletes were just not capable, because that's what history had presented, and that's the way it was going to be going forward.

To me, as a military leader, this was like allowing my enemy battle space and control Of the theater of operations simply because of their presence. Not because they had superior numbers, better weapons, or more numbers, or some other tactical or strategic advantage. It made no sense to me, and it was the athletes who were suffering the consequences from a lack of leadership within the weak team culture that had developed.

Keep in mind, this rival school is located in the adjacent town, only 20 minutes away. They don't drink from a magical water well. Their student body basically comes from the same genetic stock as ours. And their school is actually smaller than ours, so the talent pool is not the factor either. Why then, have they been so successful, so dominant, and we have not? Well, when boiled down, it revealed one thing as their significant advantage over us (and frankly, many other programs in the state as well), and that is their culture. It was so obvious to me that we must establish a winning and successful culture in order to compete with them (and all the other programs) and by doing so, we would become a winning and successful program as a result.

When you ask my athletes about our program, they will commonly say that it resembles more a family than just being a sports team. This is an extraordinary description to have established this new cultural paradigm in such a short time.

So, how did I do it? Well it kind of falls in line with the 'making chicken salad' theory as culture is a critical ingredient of making something good from preexisting components and then taking it to a greater level from that point.

The model that I use to establish our program culture is not secretive nor rocket science. In fact, it has been around since 1943. It is structured and certainly does not involve luck. It is all about creating the proper environment where your team members will reach their optimum performance, or within this model, self-actualization, their fullest potential, as athletes and teammates.

In all honesty, at its core, it is based on a basic principle of psychology called Maslow's Hierarchy of Needs. Let's go over it briefly and I think, as a coach, keeping it all within the context of you building a positive and thriving culture for your program, this makes allot of sense.

1. Physiological Needs – These are our most basic requirements to exist, air, food, water, shelter, clothing, et cetera. For us as coaches, we can leverage this to mean some very practical things like a water jug or rehydration source, the proper running gear and uniforms, a designated team meeting place or maybe a team tent during meets, a box of granola bars or some orange slices or bananas to fuel our athletes, before and after practices and meets.

2. Safety Needs – In order to perform we all must feel safe and secure, and to be healthy. As a coach, this means I need to make sure my choice of workouts and running environments are safe and responsible. I need to have a zero-tolerance for hazing and bullying. I need to be trained and prepared to respond to any medical or personal emergency. All my athletes must have a clear understanding that I am always committed to them with their best interest in mind. And, not just the top tier athletes, ALL of them.

3. Love and Belonging – Experiencing a sense of friendship, intimacy, family, and common connection is not only what I strive for my teams, but a basic human need. There are so many ways that we can encourage and stimulate these things...team dinners, movie nights, community service projects, group hikes, team chats, just to name a few things. Taking the time to communicate true compassion; listen to them, give a hug once in a while as appropriate. One unique tradition my program does is we celebrate each other and our families by having a tailgate potluck picnic after every meet. It allows everyone to just take some dedicated time to enjoy and absorb the moment that we have created together (no matter the outcome of the meet) with our teammates, coaches, and families.

4. Esteem – Feeling respect and being validated, recognized for personal contribution or efforts, feeling empowered by having the freedom to share feelings and opinions, to simply feel like a valued part of the process goes a very long way in defining your program's culture and will influence the level of success that will come from it.

I have a team rule. If someone is speaking, everyone is listening. It does not just apply to the coaches; it applies to everyone. Some of the most powerful words come from our athletes and allowing them to have a voice liberates their loyalty and reinforces their commitment to their teammates.

I also do fun and simple things to show reward for personal effort. Sometimes that means giving a box of pasta to top performers or allowing an athlete who really worked hard during our interval training to choose the next day's running route, or just a round of applause for making the honor roll. Whatever it is, everyone loves to be recognized for their contributions, large or small.

5. Self-Actualization – This is the desire to become the best that they can become. Collectively, when providing the needs of 1 thru 4, this is the place where optimum performance derives, for all the right reasons. Self-confidence, positive mindset, team pride, a purpose greater than themselves all comes from this aspect of the overall team culture that you have created.

As a coach-leader, providing this need is your responsibility and should be the consistent goal for your program. Reaching this point is where your athletes, and your team, will unlock the abilities to achieve the unachievable.

By establishing a positive culture in this way, it not only benefits your program, perhaps more deeply, it provides a proven model for a complete, empathetic, and compassionate way of life that your athletes will grasp and emulate in some way going forward.

As I have said, and will continue to believe, leading as a coach is NOT about YOU, it is about how you impact those around you in a way that will make those you influence better humans, and as a result, this world a better place. That, in its essence, is the profound importance of the culture that you are responsible for creating.

SECTION II –

We Are Who We Think We Are

> "*Victorious warriors win first and then go to war, while defeated warriors go to war first and then seek to win.*"
>
> -Sun Tzu

In this section of the book, I would like to take some time to have a dedicated conversation about the power and importance of mindset. It is true, 'we are who we think we are', and our behaviors reflect those beliefs. This is not to say that our physical preparation, our training plans, our strategy development, our administrative work, and all the other physical and action-oriented elements that go into building a successful program are any less important. However, those things are more transactional in nature. Mindset is the element that allows our teams to take those transactional pieces and put them to work collectively to institute the purpose, perception, and the ability to believe that one can achieve the unachievable, individually and collectively. Having the right attitude and fortitude is often the difference maker that levels the playing field or offers the competitive advantage that separates the bad from the good, and the good from the great.

That having been said, allow me to share some of the key mindset subjects that I actively and openly present, promote, and development as a coach and leader.

PEAK PERFORMANCE

◆ ◆ ◆

The secret to peak performance as an individual or as a team, no matter the arena or environment, is performing in a mindset of purpose greater than one's self. I keep saying, "it's NOT about YOU", as a coach or as an athlete, or whatever your role in life. If you want to perform as a top-notch coach and you want your athletes to perform at their highest levels, then a establishing a mindset of purpose will generate inspiration that results in overall peak performance.

I often like to frame a base sense of purpose within a greater scope of priority. For instance, I talk to my teams about who we represent and why we exist. "Why do we wear the same uniforms?", is a question I ask to open the conversation. The basic answer that I am seeking is that we represent each other, our school, our families, and the communities that make up our school. As we compete against larger schools, we represent all the smaller schools, and when we go and compete out of state, we represent our state.

When framing purpose as a big-picture mentality that is greater than us as individuals, it takes an individualist selfish mindset and begins to refocus it as a selfless one.

This is not a one-time speech within my program, it is something that I embrace and reinforce consistently. Sometimes it's simple verbal reinforcement, but also I support it with action by expecting our upperclassmen to support and interact with our underclass athletes, I expect my more elite to actively encourage and run with the less talented members of their team.

Demonstrating genuine mutual respect and thoughtfulness is a requirement to remain on the team roster. I fully understand that not all people are compatible, and I do not expect everyone to be best friends, but I do expect everyone to get along all for the common good of the team and what we represent. Besides, isn't this the lesson you want them to bring forward into their school community and then into society? I mean, that is our jobs as coaches, right? To prepare and teach important lesson of life through the microcosm of our sport.

I also expect our team captains and other leaders to organize or get involved in a meaningful community service function. This really brings clarity to the point that this world of ours is greater than any one individual, yet as individuals (alone or collectively) we can make a difference in our greater world around us.

It is critical that you reinforce this mindset because something will happen when the reality, the pain, the mental challenges, the crappy weather, the terrain, the pressure of expectation, and all the other elements of the realities of competition come crashing down on the shoulders of each athlete, or you as their coach.

You will either embrace your greater purpose as inspiration to perform and get through those challenges, or you will just go through the motions of the event, uninspired and finish with a sense of pointlessness and dissatisfaction. Because accomplishing something for someone or something else greater than you is way more meaningful than just doing it for you… every time, without fail.

This was never more evident then when I was in combat as a US Army Soldier serving in Iraq as a senior medic.

I had been a member of the US Army for nearly 20 years, on the verge of retirement eligibility. I had been called and mobilized for military missions at least eight other times, all of which ended up being cancelled or aborted. I had received orders to be deployed on a mission that was rather benign, and comparatively speaking, fairly safe. However, it wasn't long before command reached out to me and asked if I would accept another mission, a much more dangerous one, in the heart of an active combat zone. Literally, in less than five seconds of thought, I said yes.

Why would I do that when I had dodged so many high-risk deployments throughout my career and I could simply show up to my original assignment, go through the motions, serve in a low-risk environment, and then come home likely unscathed, and retire?

Because my service in the new mission option was more impactful and its purpose was so much greater. So, after those five seconds of deliberation, I said, "Yes, I'll go". And I went, to serve my country, defend freedom and establish peace, in hopes that my children or grandchildren would not have to do the same in the future, and to save lives that otherwise would not be saved.

And, when the rockets and mortar rounds fell, and the bullets began to fly, why did I run towards the fight and not away from it? For the same reasons, someone else or something else greater than me and my own safety inspired me to act at a level of peak performance that otherwise I would have never attained. It was my mindset of greater service that allowed me to achieve at levels that before were unachievable.

In fact, I am not writing this book strictly for my own benefit. Of course I have a personal dream and goal to write this book, but what actually has inspired me to do it, to share my thoughts and advantages of my successes, is the intent and hope that perhaps it will make a greater difference beyond my own scope of influence. If more coaches, more leaders, read it, learn from my lessons, and employ some of these proven philosophies in their own unique ways, then the satisfaction comes from the greater purpose and goal of making this world a better place. Are you starting to pick up what I'm laying down?

THE WARRIOR MENTALITY

◆ ◆ ◆

As a retired military man, it is quite natural for me to understand, accept, and promote what I call a 'warrior mentality'.

This mindset has nothing to do with war or violence, or anything sinister associated with those acts. It simply is an analogic attitude that supports ideals of courage, mental toughness and perseverance, loyalty, and self-discipline. These types of warrior ideals are often seen associated with sports teams and athletes who have overcome tremendous odds, people who have survived great illness or injury, and even societies and cultures that have surpassed the tests of time and insurmountable struggle.

Warriors fight side by side with each other and for each other. Warriors are resolved to succeed and overcome any battle or challenge for each other. Warriors keep going, keep moving forward until their destination is met or their goals are achieved...or they fail trying. It is the essence of competitiveness.

The point is, the warrior mentality is a positive mindset based on mental toughness and perseverance, all for the right reasons of developing personal attributes that will define achievability and survivability within the arena of sport or the world of life. Let me remind you, as a coach, you are obligated to walk that walk too. You must lead with a warrior spirit initiative if you expect your teams to act the same way. Here are some attributes of the Warrior Mentality:

Integrity - I present integrity to my athletes as doing the right thing when no one is watching. It is the content and reflection of your personal character. It is respect and compassion, mindfulness for others. Integrity allows for good sportsmanship and grace when winning or losing.

Loyalty – Being loyal is acting in a way that represents unfettered belief and confidence in your teammates, coaches, the team, and its culture.

Self-Discipline – Self-control, especially during times of high pressure, high stakes, and high emotions. It is being patient and actively introspective. This is where employing emotional intelligence can be critical to an outcome.

Accountability and Responsibility –

Being accountable and responsible go hand in hand. Holding yourself to a standard and accepting the consequences of your actions, good, bad, or indifferent, is a critical component of earning respect and acceptance especially within a team setting.

Courageousness – Looking your fear directly in its eyes, being brave. Standing up to difficult and challenging moments despite your fears. Being scared yet stepping forward into the fray, especially for the betterment of your team or on behalf of a teammate.

Camaraderie – The strong sense of belonging in unity, particularly to a team or culture. It is the reason why you will stand shoulder to shoulder with your fellow warriors providing unwavering support. It is team spirit and mindset of being in it together at its finest.

Determination - Having the will and

self-confidence to stand up to a challenge. It is undying resolve and possessing a never give up attitude. In sport, we call this competitiveness. Warriors keep moving forward no matter what.

After reviewing these warrior attributes, can you see how this mindset would make your team stronger and your athletes more effective in their efforts? It is an intangible advantage that will create tangible results and so often the reason why performance benchmarks that were once seen as unachievable can now be achieved.

YOUR WORST COMPETITION

◆ ◆ ◆

I have seen it time and time again whether it be an athlete, an employee, a soldier, and yes, even myself as a leader. Our worst competition comes from within. Look in the mirror, YOU are the only one holding yourself back from achieving the unachievable. It is the invisible thoughts and limiting preconceptions of yourself and your abilities that are holding you back from a breakthrough.

As a coach, it is your challenge to keep athletes in a positive frame of mind, out of their own limited headspace, that allows for the self-confidence and belief that they are limitless. Understanding the following principles and themes will help:

Resistance – Bestselling author, Steven Pressfield, has coined the term and describes resistance in his book, The War of Art, in this way, "Resistance cannot be seen, touched, heard, or smelled. But it can be felt. We experience it as an energy field radiating from a work-in-potential. It's a repelling force. It's negative. Its aim is to shove us away, distract us, prevent us from doing our work."

Resistance most often presents itself as the little voice in the back of your head that whispers discouragement in your ear. "You're not good enough." "You can't possibly run at that pace." "It hurts, slow down!" "You suck." It is not selective. Everyone experiences the negative influence of resistance.

Admittedly, when deciding to write this book, resistance whispered in my ear too, "Who are you to write a book and give coaching advice? No one will want to listen to you." I fight against resistance every time that I think about sitting in front of my keyboard to write. It is relentless.

The thing about resistance is that it would not exist if you did not have a dream or vision for yourself. Resistance validates your dream by its very presence. And oddly, it becomes stronger and more present the closer that you get to achieving your vision and dream. When this happens, find strength in the resistance and allow it to drive you forward. Lean into it, keep pushing, keep moving, you are almost there!

Mediocrity – Let's be real, mediocrity is a choice. It is a standard of mindset and has nothing to do with the availability of resources or circumstance, and everything to do with you, or your athletes, accepting a lesser work ethic and lazy level of dedication to achieve. You cannot just show up, unprepared and unfocused, without purpose and expectation, and expect excellence to occur.

The bottom line is that you, and your athletes, will get out of it what they put into it. For you, as a coach, it means do the work out of practice so your athletes can do the work during practice. Communicate and connect. Make expectations clear and demand effort. Reward the effort not simply their presence. A 'just show up' habit will never result in reaching the highest heights of personal or team potential.

Faith – Having faith is realizing a steadfast belief. Even during the most uncertain and questionable moments, it is the undaunting trust that knowing deep inside this is where you can turn when there is no other option. It is the right way. You feel it and know it.

Faith allows you to battle resistance, it is what keeps you diligent and moving forward. For some, faith stems from their spiritual or religious ideologies. their families, their team, and their coaches. Faith is the firewall between total self-destruction and a way to keep moving forward.

Faith is the epitome of self-confidence especially when all things seem like they are coming unhinged and defeat is inevitable. A mindset of real faith can never be broken, and it will get you through those tough times. It breeds determination and allows you to keep going, to keep moving forward, and to never give up.

Control What You Can Control – Despite faith, encouragement, and positive mindset, it is inevitable that you and your athletes will be exposed to what may seem as insurmountable disappointment and challenging circumstances. You cannot avoid it, but you can react in a way that allows you to get through it, and often, it will reveal an elemental positive side effect. Sun Tzu, who authored the anciet book, "The Art of War", says, "In the midst of chaos, there is also opportunity".

During times of uncertainty and chaos, it is essential that you find stability, the firm ground the allows you and your athletes to keep standing and withstand the storm. There are simply times that you will not be able to resist or fight against it and you will have no choice but acceptance. In fact, fighting back may only make things worse or turn out to be a colossal waste of time and effort.

The good news is, you do not need to necessarily nor completely succumb to the circumstance. Moving forward or creating a sense of moving forward is critical. So, instead of trying to control what you have no influence on, put your energy into controlling what you can control within the circumstance.

Face it, coaching can be a lonely place and it doesn't feel much more lonely as when you are in the spotlight, on the pedestal of leadership, when everyone is looking at you for guidance, direction, and encouragement. And this happens especially during moments of adversity.

I think the most vivid of examples is what has recently happened within the arena of athletics during the COVID-19 pandemic.

Amongst the chaos of fear and misinformation came comprehensive closures of schools and cancelation of sports programs. In New Hampshire, we initially remained hopeful that we could at least salvage our Spring outdoor track season. The New Hampshire Interscholastic Athletic Association, and our school administrators, were doing a good job trying to balance the realities of the situation with the emotional pressures to overreact as it presented itself locally. They managed their decision-making in a progressive manner and maintained a sense of optimism for the athletes.

However, once the State government determined that schools were to close and students remain distanced from one another indefinitely, the Spring sports season was put on hold indefinitely. This greatly affected our program and the positive momentum that we had worked so diligently on establishing over the previous two years. Emotions were high, parents and athletes were angry and sad, and feelings of disbelief and uncertainty were real and present. It was chaos and it was threatening all that our program stood for because it felt like our program, our team, and our purpose was also taken away when the season was lost.

As the coach, especially with my experience leading during times of distress and confusion, I knew that it was my responsibility to step up and lead my athletes, their parents, and whoever else was paying attention through the fray.

During any crisis. A leader must be mindful to look around and see the situation for what it is, and how to best react to it. It does not even need to be the best decision at the time, but the action of making a decision that leads things forward, is better than inaction...every single time.

A leader must determine what she can change and what she cannot, and do not dwell and waste time, effort, and emotional investment on the things that cannot be changed. In other words, control what you can control.

In this circumstance I needed to remain connected, maintain some form of normalcy, and provide athletes, especially my Seniors, an empathetic and listening ear, and sense of purpose. This was challenging since we were not allowed to meet or "coach" our teams in any way.

Within minutes after the announcement was made to postpone spring sports, I was inundated with questions from distraught kids. The athletes and some parents reached to me for direction and encouragement. There was no way that I was going to leave them hanging in the mess and confusion.

Meanwhile, despite having been put

on indefinite hold, there was still hope that a modified season could occur once the government's pandemic restrictions were lifted. It was the opportunity to lead. After all, I had learned that when there is a crisis, leaders must lead. My athletes needed direction and structure, they needed something that they could identify as normalcy while their world was crumbling around them.

First, it was imperative that we stay connected. Without connection and communication nothing else would matter. If I could have had a team meeting, I would have but since that was out of my control, I used our established social media platforms and team text message group to stay in contact. I was very transparent and shared news about the situation in real time as it developed. I also took the time to reach out directly to the Seniors to listen, validate their feelings, and ensure them that they were not alone in thier disappointment and anger.

Next, I provided the seniors a conitnued sense of team and purpose by breaking down the team roster into smaller training groups and asked the seniors to be team leaders for these groups. We, the coaches, provided training guidance, resources, and motivation. I depended on the seniors to lead this training since coaches were prohibited from actively engaging our teams. Despite the final decision about our season, they could keep moving forward.

They were controlling what they could control with structure and purpose. And no matter the outcome, they would have no regret and retain the positive satisfaction of accomplishing what they could instead of dwelling on the negativity of what they couldn't. And, if the season did resume, we would be ready. Worst case scenario was that the season would be completely cancelled (as it was), yet even still, they had contributed to the development of their underclass teammates and the season was not a total loss. It was their valuable contribution to the future of the program and through that they remain as a vital part of its legacy.

'Control what you can control' is such a relevant theory as a coach, and a crucial lesson to teach your athletes. Your athletes commonly experience moments of chaos or what might feel as overwhelming circumstances, especially during competition or everyday life as a student and young person. Teaching them to take a breath, look around and evaluate the situation, control what they can, and disengage from what they cannot is a universal skill that they can take with them and utilize the rest of their lives.

HOPE IS NOT A STRATEGY

◆ ◆ ◆

As a coach, being strategic is vital to your success and effectiveness. Whether you are preparing for the next season, planning for a specific meet, taking over a program, or reinventing your current program, without having a strategic plan you are throwing your opportunity for success into the winds of chance and hoping positive outcome will blow your way.

There is one thing that I have learned in my many years as an organizational leader, coach, military non-commissioned officer, and an executive director. Hope is not a strategy.

As a leader of your team, it is your responsibility and obligation to be deliberate in your coaching. Not creating and applying a strategy plays into the 'just show up' mentality that 'mediocrity is a choice'...it is your choice.

When I think of strategy, some rules of thumb come to mind immediately:

Be Deliberate

Planning and applying your strategy are like constructing a pyramid. It must have a broad base and it concludes with a pointed objective. Be deliberate and write out the plan. Create the blueprint for your success. Can you imagine what would have happened if the ancient pyramids were built without blueprints and planning? Likely, they would never have been completed.

There was a saying in the military that

was said often, "Plan your work and work your plan." So, start planning. Your vision and goals for your program are a good place to start. That vision and those goals can be lofty, but they should be based on reality as you see it. In other words, they must be attainable within reason. The resources, talents, and support afforded to you and your program should be considered when developing a realistic strategy. Sometimes it is actually easier to plan backwards. Start with your goals at the top and build it backwards to the base of your vision. Fill in the building blocks of your pyramid with the specifics of how you are going to take your vision and make it the reality of your goals. You can do this for your entire season, a particular meet, or even your daily training.

There is something else to keep in mind once you have your plan in place. Be flexible within your strategy because change is inevitable. Yup, shit happens, it's a fact of life. I always say, "Have a plan C, because your Plan B can become your Plan A in a heartbeat", and then you will be ready to keep going. Always consider risks and contingencies when strategizing. Your strategy should be not a secret, at least within the confines of your program. Include other key stakeholders when developing it and share it with your team members. Remember the discussion point of inclusivity? Ownership and clarity will bring a higher level of outcome every single time.

Challenge History and Be a Visionary

Be courageous and dream big. Understand what the history of your program has been within the school's accomplishments over time. Use those moments to help create your vision, realistic expectations, goals, and challenges for your program's strategy.

At my current school, our cross country program has never won a state championship, but it has for Track and Field. It is quite clear to me what my vision is for my program. To make school history and bring home the first cross country State championship and the next Track and Field title!

Now, how I get there and make that vision a reality is in the specifics of the strategy itself and includes every component of coaching that this book has covered, plus training and racing components too. Writing it down makes it real and brings clarity to your strategy.

Know Your Opponent

As you create your strategic plan, be it long term for your program, or short term for a specific meet, it is important to understand what challenges that you may face. What will be your opposition and subsequent risks within your strategy and how will you prepare for them? Consideration of these influential elements and building in successive plans and contingencies will add strength to your strategies. Do the homework that will provide you the best information from which to create your strategy. Your strategy should not only be strong it should be smart. So be smart when creating it.

ACHIEVING THE UNACHIEVABLE

❖ ❖ ❖

Every Season, I have an organizational team meeting that includes all the athletes, returning veterans and newcomers. I also hold a separate organizational meeting for the Parents. I welcome everyone, we do introductions, speak about team expectations and logistics, share a story or two, maybe even tell a joke and have some laughs.

The one thing that I have begun to do is provide a promise to everyone on the team. Admittedly, it is a big and bold promise but since I have committed to doing it, it has been a promise that has been upheld with 100% certainty.

It goes like this, "I promise that if you fully commit to this team as much as I am committed to it, that you will achieve something that prior to this day you believed was unachievable".

Now, definitively this promise is real, substantive, and quantitative. This is simply not about feeling accomplished, although that is part of it, but it is about achieving real achievements as a team and as an individual athlete. It is personal and collective all at the same time and it commonly applies to each and every team member without exception.

It is also not about winning, at least in the traditional sense. So, I think it is important that we discuss and define winning in terms of winning versus discovering victory through achievement.

I really want to be clear here. I love to win! I am ferociously competitive! There is nothing I want more for my team than to be the best they can be but I do not allow my burning desire to win, or my own warrior mentality as a competitor to cloud my understanding of what winning is really about. It is not necessarily about the simple transaction of having the top score, defeating an opponent, bringing home the trophy or medals, or hanging that championships banner. All that is great reward but winning is really about discovering true victory and that is so often not winning the race, the meet, or the title.

I discovered early on in my coaching career that winning is a by-product of effort and effective strategy. It is the cumulative effect of the process and relationships between coach and athletes. Basically, everything that we have discussed together in this book.

Undoubtedly, I realize that there will be skeptics out there, and they will say or think that I am simply justifying the fact that I have never led a team to win a team championship as a coach and that is the weakness within my philosophies.

The fact that I have not yet won a team championship is true but it has never been because of flawed beliefs or practices. I have come so close on so many heart-breaking occasions but not yet accomplished this feat. It is the final check mark on my list of personal goals as a coach. It will allow the circle to close, much like serving my country in combat fulfilled every goal I had as a military leader in the United States Army. None the less, I have been a part of incredible and inspiring accomplishments at both the individual and team levels. Accomplishments that otherwise never would have occured. I have been blessed to be associated with many personal records, school records, state champions, All-American performances, scholarship winners, national and regional accomplishments...all unachievable achievements created as the by-products of the 'Coach E' process, in several sports at every level. That's why I know this philosophy of mine works, and perhaps that's why it is so frustrating that I have not yet won a team championship (as of the publication of this book).

There are some great coaches out there who have never won a championship at the highest level. Relatively speaking, I am in amazing company and I find some solace in that fact. In the NFL there's Marv Levy of the Buffalo Bills who went to the Superbowl four times but never won.

There are Brad Stevens and Mark few, basketball coaches who brought their teams to the NCAA finals and lost. I could create a list as long as my arm. I just do not want to be on a list like that.

I really do not want to believe that it is a selfish goal but Perhaps stems from my competitive nature, or that winning a championship is the gold-standard that everyone else recognizes as being succesful, or perhaps it's the validation of simply feeling that my career is complete and I have reached the proverbial mountain top of the coaching world. Winning a championship really is the only achievement left for me yet to achieve as a coach for my athletes.

Despite this fact, and despite that winning a team championship has become a major goal that continues to drive me individually, I cannot allow myself to get caught up in the transaction of simply winning for the sake of chasing a personal dream and fulfilling a selfish goal. It's tough not to fall into this trap, but after all, I continue to remind myself that coaching is not about me... and it's definitely not about the "w's" that we as coaches collect along the way.

Recently, I had one of the most honest conversations with my athletic director about where I am as a coach. It was my annual employee review and despite being a veteran coach, I embraced the opportunity to hear his perspectives and learn from his observations of my collective weaknesses and strengths. By doing this, it promotes personal and professional growth and helps to refocus my mindset and improve my effectiveness as a coach and leader.

The conversation went like this, "Bill, you are a great coach. You have done some unbelievable things for our students in such a short time at our school. But if there is one thing that I see for you to improve it's your emphasis on winning the banner." He continued, "Don't get me wrong, winning a state championship is awesome, but don't let it distract you from the real victories of your program and your kids. Those victories come from the journey, not the destination."

You know, he was exactly right. As much as winning is a by-product of the effort, victory, at any level, is found within the journey of the effort. This was a profound reminder and re-aligning moment for me. Perhaps in an underlying way, is one of the main reasons why I decided to write this book. With this book, I can publicly hold myself accountable to recognizing the victories of this journey and remind myself that it is not about me.

As such, it is about my athletes and what they can take away from my programs and philosophies that they otherwise would not have received, gained, or earned elsewhere. It is up to me to inspire them, motivate them, care about them, support them, have fun with them, and celebrate with them.

In the end, it is creating the lasting impact beyond our current connection that will give them the courage and confidence to have goals, recognize their victories along their journeys, overcome challenges, and continue to do the unthinkable in life and fulfill their own promise...to **achieve the unachievable**.

ACKNOWLEDGEMENT

◆ ◆ ◆

Quotation References:

Steven Pressfield, **The War of Art** - Break Through the Blaocks and Win Your Inner Creative Battles, Black Irish Entertainment, New York, 2002.

Sun Tzu, **The Art of War**, an ancient Chinese military treatise dating from the Late Spring and Autumn Period, (roughly 5th centruty BC).

Special Gratitude:

I would like to thank all of my current and former coaching colleagues who have always believed in my philospohioes and practices, and who have always made me a better coach and leader.

Also thank you to my past coaches, who have always taught me by their example, good or bad. Fortunately, the positive coaches in my life planted the seed of my passion. This specifically refers to my Dad, Richard Edson, as my little League Baseball coach, Jim Cunningham as my High School Cross Country Coach, and Tom Stricker my High School Track & Field Coach.

I must also acknowledge the positive impact of my family, whom without, I would have absolutely no purpose to live. I love you all!

And Finally, I must acknowledge my Lord and Savior, Jesus Christ. To God be the glory for all things I accomplish.

ABOUT THE AUTHOR

Bill Edson

Bill Edson has been a successful athletics coach for nearly three decades and has had the privilege of coaching thousands of athletes at every level from youth sports through collegiate athletics. He maintains a Bachelor of Art degree in Professional Studies and Organizational Leadership with a concentration in human behavior, a Master of Science degree in Organizational Leadership, a Post-graduate Diploma in Sports Psychology and Peak Performance, and many other coaching profession certifications. He is a retired Senior Non-Commissioned Officer of the United States Army where he has been highly decorated for his leadership and significant contributions to the Army's medical mission during peacetime and combat operations. Bill also has spent ten years as a transformational executive leader in the non-profit business sector. Coaching cross country and track & field at the interscholastic level is his passion where he most recently has transformed the boys and girls teams at Conant High School to be one of the top emerging programs in the State of New Hampshire. He resides in Peterborough with his wife, Carol, and their rescue dog, Birdie. Together, they have five children and five grandchildren.

www.ingramcontent.com/pod-product-compliance
Lightning Source LLC
Chambersburg PA
CBHW050007230526
45465CB00003BB/1300